RECKLESS SURRENDER

RECKLESS SURRENDER

YOU ARE ONE DECISION AWAY FROM FULFILLING YOUR PURPOSE ON THIS EARTH

BETH PACKARD

TALL PINE

Reckless Surrender

Copyright © 2019 by Beth Packard

All rights reserved solely by the author. The author guarantees all contents are original and do not infringe upon the legal rights of any other person or work. No part of this book may be reproduced in any form without the permission of the author. The views expressed in this book are not necessarily those of the publisher.

Scripture quotations marked TPT are from The Passion Translation®. Copyright © 2017, 2018 by Passion & Fire Ministries, Inc. Used by permission. All rights reserved. ThePassionTranslation.com.

ISBN-13: 9781693565359

Tall Pine Books: An Imprint of Pulpit to Page
|| tallpinebooks.com
|| pulpittopage.com

"Beth Packard attended one of my *Release the Writer* seminars in Oklahoma City. Being a fellow "PK" (preacher's kid) we connected. Two years later, I was excited to receive a draft of this manuscript in my inbox. She did it! She had crossed the finish line and was ready to share her story with you.

In *Reckless Surrender*, Beth is open about being closed off by religion; something I believe will resonate with many readers. She shares God's pursuit of her as He drew her into a relationship and caught her up in love. This outrageous love she has for those to whom she is called is infectious and inviting. Full of personal stories, encouragement, and faith, Beth's book provides a clear call for you—enter in."

—Wendy K. Walters
Mentor, Minister, Motivator, Master Coach
Author of *Intentionality* and *Marketing Your Mind*

"Did you know that God has a wild side? And did you know that His wild side is wildly pursuing you? For ages I believe God has been wooing humanity into a deep encounter with Himself. In a world that craves authenticity, my friend, Beth Packard, writes as a tried and tested voice that has been touched by the affection of our Father.

Reckless Surrender removes the veil of lies we believe pertaining to the goodness of God. In it, we discover a Father who passionately loves us yet jealously seeks our full devotion. I heartily endorse this book as I believe it is not only a timely message to our generation, but also a cry to return to our first love."

—Alex Parkinson
Mirrorimageintl.com
Author of *Partakers of The Divine*

"The thing that makes someone's story or testimony so powerful is *relatability*. As I read *Reckless Surrender*, I was so moved, because there are so many people stuck in powerless religion. This book will reveal to many; to the lost and the prodigals, that the gospel is not a story, but a person, Jesus Christ. God truly desires for us to know Him and He longs to reveal Himself in all His fullness. As you read, you will be taken on a journey into the fire of God's love! May you come to know Him in a deeper way! That His love is real, tangible, that He is an all consuming fire!"

—Jesse Shamp
Kingdom Culture International
Co-author of *Miracles in the Glory*

DEDICATION & ACKNOWLEDGEMENTS

I dedicate this book to all the forerunners of our faith, thank you for plowing!! I thank you, Holy Spirit, for never giving up on me, and continually pursuing me. Thank you for showing me the path of such reckless surrender before my Lord Jesus.

To my husband, Aaron, my chosen one—I love and honor you. Thank you for your dedication to our marriage and our children: Luke, Grace & Lydia. Thank you Aaron for chasing after Jesus with ALL your heart! Thank you for lifting me up and giving me a voice beside you to walk in my Kingdom Destiny!

To my dearest friends who have encouraged me through endless hours on this journey of writing. You are a treasure, and I couldn't have done this without you. Jamie and Marolyn—you two especially have never wavered, and have blessed me abundantly! (Prov. 18:24)

To my Editor and amazing sister, Angela, thank you for the phenomenal help on this project and for always looking out for me! Michelle, thank you for your insight, wisdom and love during this process.

To the numerous friends and family who held my head up and encouraged me to dive deep into the powerful supernatural realm of God, thank you! You sowed into good soil! I am forever grateful.

Lastly, to my Dad and Mom and dear in-laws, your prayers endured through many years! We are so blessed to have such loving parents partnered with us as we preach the Kingdom throughout the nations!

CONTENTS

Foreword	1
Introduction	3
1. Reckless Pursuit	9
2. A Father's Reckless Love	17
3. Reckless Surrender	25
4. Reckless Obedience	33
5. Reckless Abandon	39
6. Recklessly Pursue the Promised Land	47
7. Practical Steps and Decrees to Enter into the Promised Land	53
Connect with Beth	63

FOREWORD

Reckless. Now there's a word to describe Beth Packard. When I first met her, I felt immediately at home. She invites you into her life wholeheartedly with no regrets. I've watched her interact with her family and observed a woman who gives all. She lifts up her husband, homeschools their three children, runs a ministry, business, and church, and hosts a podcast, "Super-Natural Living with Beth Packard," all while giving her everything to Jesus. She is all in.

And I suspect you will find that same thing in these pages. Beth gives to you, just like her family, an open heart. She lays before you a tapestry of love and grace that, no doubt, came from the inevitable interwoven struggles that life brings. If you need a foundation in which to build the next platform of your life, I pray that you will find it here. A foundation of hope, courage, and strength will meet you face to face.

I find myself wanting to dive deeper in God after reading this book. Beth renewed a childlike faith in me and reminded me that I am truly living "the greatest love story." After all the years in ministry and traveling around the world to preach the Good News of Jesus Christ, I've never been more convinced of this fact: The greatest mystery is the love of Jesus. Knowing His love is my ultimate mission. If I find it, if I encounter it, then I have successfully lived.

I want to invite you to go on this journey. Reach out and take Beth's hand and let her show you her world. Let her give you all her heart as she so longingly desires to give. Let her voice fill your sails and let the wind blow where it wills. Give in, lean back, and become a life of *Reckless Surrender*.

—Jennifer Martin
Co-Founder of *Contagious Love International*
Host of *Awaken the Heart Saturation Sessions*
www.contagiousloveintl.com

INTRODUCTION

"The source of revelation-knowledge is found as you fall down in surrender before the Lord. Don't expect to see the Shekinah glory until the Lord sees your sincere humility."
—*Proverbs 16:33 TPT*

I grew up in the church—a preacher's kid, actually. As a teenager, I used to count the tiles on the ceiling in the church and beg God to close the mouth of the pastor (my dad) so we could finally go eat lunch. (I love you so much, Dad. Thank you for never giving up on me!) Looking back, it was a tremendous burden to not know God intimately at that point in my life. The day to day was such a chore, and seriously, it was hard work to behave and always do the "right" thing in my own strength. Actually, I miserably failed at it. Strive, fail. Strive, fail, Strive, fail. Can you relate?

I am a no-nonsense, straightforward, transparent,

heart-on-her-sleeve kind of gal. To fake my way through my teen years and try to fit into religion's mold was the most pathetic acting role I ever attempted. It truly was horrifying and resulted in me going the way of the world and seeking the pleasures that the world flaunted in front of me. At least there I could be who I wanted to be. Except, let's be honest, the world shaped me and molded me into its *own* image, a counterfeit of who God called me to be. I was trapped, once again, in a giant lie. I was broken and found my destiny stolen completely. The world abused me and stole so much from me. The enemy stole my passion and my heart's desires and left me cold, wet, used, and alone on the curb.

Religion, filled with rules and demands, with no help to fulfill them, made me literally sick to my stomach. Yet the world's ways brought depression and hopelessness. My passion was lost and I, quite frankly, was lost. I remember crying out to God something like, "IF YOU REALLY CARE... HELP ME!"

You see, I had given my heart to Jesus and vowed to serve Him faithfully all the days of my life at the ripe young age of five. I was baptized in a muddy Tennessee river by my daddy that same year. I had amazing Sunday school teachers who didn't just teach me about Jesus, but taught me how to be *like* Jesus. I remember my early childhood filled with joy and love, growing up in a family of six in middle Tennessee. My parents worked hard and loved the Lord and served Him faithfully, even when trials came. God asked my parents to do some really hard things. I honor them both for teaching me and being such great examples of surrendered vessels in God's hand.

As the seasons changed, I entered middle school, coinciding with a move back to Kansas. It was then I started questioning many things. I knew God was real; I never, ever questioned His existence. I simply didn't want what was being offered anymore. It wasn't what my five-year-old self signed up for, to be completely honest. I didn't have a name for it, or even understand what was happening, other than something changed. The passion had left, the fire had gone dim. Things spiraled quickly at such an impressionable age. I needed to press into Jesus and really know Him, but I just felt a religious heaviness.

I would describe religion as having knowledge of the Truth, without taking action or allowing the Truth to go deep and take root inside. Simply hearing the Word of God, but refusing to allow it to change us. To me, I perceived religion like a mask of fake, lifeless rules that had NO power to change anyone or anything. During those preteen/teen years, I felt condemned and guilty for failing over and over again. I would strive so hard in my own power, without much luck.

I didn't understand the free gift of grace that God gave me, and I chose instead to work hard to earn my good standing before Him. When that didn't work, my passion and desires, both of which God designed me uniquely to embrace, were quickly squashed in the confines of my belief system and that heavy weight of religion. I desperately desired to be unveiled and set free, just as Romans 8:19 declares: *"The entire universe is standing on tiptoe, yearning to see the unveiling of God's glorious sons and daughters!"* I simply had no idea how to do this. I was broken. I was used up. I was worn out, lost.

Please, from the bottom of my heart, I plead with you, will you go on a journey with me? If you have been hurt by religion, the church, or are just seeking real power that you haven't found anywhere before, these stories will inspire you. The pages of this book are my raw, vulnerable steps to seeking God's true nature, His presence.

This is my journey of lying on my face in a mess of my own snot and tears, begging Him to reveal Himself to me and awaken my heart again! In the following pages, you will find me asking Him to use me for something that truly matters in the light of all eternity, to light my soul on FIRE! To help me burn with passion and desire. To allow me to help set the captives free, as I live each day to its fullest. I want to leave a legacy for my children and grandchildren of what God can do through a surrendered, willing vessel.

It is my heart's desire and passion to help you, my friend, to find a place of such *reckless surrender* before the Lord, that you truly understand the Scripture, *"Whoever loses their life for My (God's) sake will find it"* (Matthew 10:39).

Do you struggle with these things? Do you hold tight to control because you are scared of the unknown? Are you stuck in a lukewarm or even dead religion? Is your heart burning for excitement, for passion to arise and set YOU free?! I believe it is! That feeling, where you want to say "Yes!" and also throw up simultaneously? Your heart pounds and you want to run the other way? Yes! That's it. Embrace it with me; it gets so much better just on the other side of that fear! There is such VICTORY in a personal relationship with the King of all kings!

> "Have I not commanded you? Be strong and courageous. Do not be afraid; do not be discouraged, for the LORD your God will be with you wherever you go." (Joshua 1:9)

In the following pages, I am going to share how God radically encountered me and transformed me. He is calling YOU, right now. I can hear Him saying to me as I write, "Lead My daughter, lead My son, on this journey I've taken you on, and help them find who I created them to be!"

Friend, we were made for this! Fear not. Be strong and courageous. Let's do this together! I'm so proud of you for taking these first steps with me! I promise you won't regret this, because the Truth always sets us free!

1

RECKLESS PURSUIT

"The spirit that God breathed into our hearts is a jealous Lover who intensely desires to have more and more of us."
—James 4:5

My heart is pounding nearly out of my chest as my eyes roam left and right, searching, without understanding. I hear a voice telling me which way to turn, as I carefully take each step on the narrow cement path. This path is my only option for survival and yet it's a maze of endless turns. Surrounding the path on all sides are intersecting paths and "DANGER: HIGH VOLTAGE" signs declaring the water below me, beside me, all around me, would end my life in an instant if I take the wrong step or lose my balance and fall.

To make matters worse, three men are in reckless pursuit of me! I am terrified! I know if they reach me, their desire is to plunge me into the electrifying currents of the water. I can *taste death, as my blood is shooting through my body at outrageous speed. I listen carefully to a voice helping me control my steps and stay safe on the path. I am doing all I can to escape my pursuers and spare my own life.*

I wake up in bed next to my husband, sweating, heart pounding. It was just a dream, except, there was something so real, so deeply moving about this "dream."

"What exactly just happened to me?" I questioned.

What an experience. I relive it each time I share the details. Have you wondered how a dream can feel so real? In the spring of 2016, I experienced the first of many dreams just like this, and I can I tell you, seeking out its meaning and purpose literally changed my life forever.

My husband, Aaron, and I had been studying and learning much about dreams and how the Holy Spirit gives us revelation, ideas, and wisdom through our nighttime hours. I was asking the Lord to speak to me and reveal secrets to me, anytime and anywhere. I believe this dream was an answer to those prayers. Seeking out what He was sharing with me, I had to understand the mysterious details of this encounter. It caused me to press into Him even more.

Throughout Scripture, time and time again, God used prophetic dreams to show His children their destinies and even save entire nations! Consider Joseph's dreams in Genesis 37. What a prophetic experience! As a boy, God showed him things to come concerning his own destiny. As he grew older, he had the opportunity to interpret

Pharaoh's dream about the nation and the coming years of plenty and years of famine (Genesis 41). Through these dreams, Joseph was able to save not only his own life, but all of Egypt and the surrounding areas from famine. Daniel also experienced the interpretation of Pharaoh's dreams (Daniel 2), which saved not only his own life, but allowed him, a godly man, to become very influential in the world's system. God truly uses our nighttime dreams to speak into our destiny and our callings. He uses any means He can in order to speak to us.

The morning following this dream, I shared the details with my husband and also a family friend who had been helping us a great deal with interpreting dreams. Our friend prayed like Daniel did for wisdom and an interpretation for me. We had his insight from the Lord, and further revelation from our own prayer time, asking God to confirm and reveal more to me. We sensed a connection with the heart of God on what He was sharing with me through this dream. The interpretation should not have surprised me, and yet it did. It was a perfect reflection of my heart at that moment in my life.

The three pursuers in the dream were not *actually* my enemies, but each of the three represented God the Father, Jesus, and the Holy Spirit. Do you recall how I was running from them, terrified? You can say at this point in my walk, I was certainly a little apprehensive about releasing full control of my life and surrendering everything to God. I believe those waters surrounding me represented the energizing waters of the Holy Spirit (John 7:37-39). The voice I was listening to for direction was unfortunately a very common result of being led by fear; the voice was that of the enemy of my soul, Satan.

Do you realize the enemy will guide us and direct us, through fear, far from our greatest calling and God's perfect will for us? Satan was keeping me from the ONE thing that could truly set me free, those cleansing, healing, life giving (high voltage) waters. Those waters would indeed kill my flesh and simultaneously awaken my spirit to the supernatural realm. Submerged in those waters my analytical mind would be still, FINALLY, and God's Holy Spirit could truly have His way in me. There was no clearer response: to fully be His, I must fully lose my own life.

> "For if you choose to self-sacrifice and lose your life for my glory, you will continually discover true life. But if you choose to keep your life for yourself, you will forfeit what you try to keep." (Matthew 16:25)

God's reckless pursuit of me was not "just a dream." This encounter radically changed my life. The love behind a pursuit so personal to me was overwhelming. For the King of the universe to involve Himself in my nighttime dreams, to speak to me, to make Himself known to me, was overwhelming, powerful, and left me feeling deeply loved and adored. I was terrified in the dream, running from God, thinking I would lose everything if I was caught. But He has shown me, while that IS true, He has something incomparably better for me in exchange for my old life. To be totally honest, I didn't even care much for my old life, so why was I so concerned about exchanging it for something incredible?

Do you know the King of the entire universe is pursuing you just the same way? He will never stop pursuing you and me. It is, in fact, His greatest desire to be intimate with us. He actually yearns for us; He longs for us intently! *"The Spirit that God breathed into our hearts is a jealous Lover who intensely desires to have more and more of us"* (James 4:5). As He pursues us, it is our job to respond. We must respond in order to come into relationship with Him.

Throughout the Scriptures, we see God pursuing men and women. John Bevere states, "This has been God's heart cry throughout the ages! A people who would desire to know Him in response to His desire for us! Genesis tells us, 'Enoch walked with God' (Gen. 5:24); 'Noah walked with God' (Gen. 6:9). We witness this again with Abraham when God invites him to 'walk before me' (Gen. 17.1). This invitation is extended again and again with Isaac and Jacob; even before Jacob was born, God said, 'Jacob I have loved' (Rom. 9:13). The Lord pursued him, as He does with us all, even when Jacob was not pursuing God" (*Drawing Near*, p. 13).

During the pursuit in the dream, do you remember

the fear I felt? I was listening so intently to the voice of the enemy simply out of fear. Fear of the unknown, fear of losing my life, fear of being out of control. I was engaging this fear and allowing it to control me.

I heard Robby Dawkins once say the fear we feel when a situation arises is not actually "our" fear, but it's the fear of our enemy. Scripture tells us in 2 Timothy 1:7a, *"For God will never give you the spirit of fear but the Holy Spirit who gives you mighty power, love and self-control."* If you think about it, Satan fears us being obedient to the Lord. There is possibly nothing Satan fears more than you and me walking in our destiny and pressing through these fears to find true freedom in Christ! If you and I have not been given a spirit of fear, the very essence of fear belongs to the enemy.

This was a powerful revelation to me, knowing the more fear I feel, the more intense the promise is of peace as I choose to obey God. The more terrifying a situation, the more desperate we are for God to show up and be our Comforter. The Holy Spirit is called the Comforter for a reason. Many times, we don't want to be uncomfortable, and we seldom experience Him because there is no need for Him. We align all our ducks and make sure we have secured our future in our own strength. He calls us to do something uncomfortable and we cringe and pretend it wasn't Him who asked. Or we ask for five more confirmations, hoping He finds someone else to answer the call. I've been there. How about you?

What areas do you need to press through right now, today? How will your destiny be released as you lay fear aside and obey the call God has placed on your life? What if you put your own security aside, ruffled a few feathers, and said "Yes!" to Him? What if you laughed in the face of fear? What if you FULLY walked in the Holy Spirit who gives you mighty power, love, and self-control?

Right now, I renounce the spirit of fear that is plaguing you, in Jesus' name, and decree and declare you will walk in courage and boldness, and you will not fear the terror of this world, but you will take refuge in the shelter of the Most High, and rest in the shadow of the Almighty (Psalm 91).

2

A FATHER'S RECKLESS LOVE

"The greatest day of our lives is when we deny ourselves, become truly free of ourselves, and become Love." —**Pastor Dan Mohler**

Wow, what does that love look like? Are you familiar with the popular Christian song, "Reckless Love" by Cory Asbury?

The lyrics dive into the beginning of Creation, before we were even formed. God was breathing life into us and pursuing us, drawing us back into intimacy with Him. He went so far as to send His own Son—His one and only Son—to restore our perfect relationship that was lost during the fall of man in Genesis 3. I've heard my husband explain it this way: God literally bankrupted Heaven; He gave all that it had. Jesus left His throne and entered the world as a baby to become our perfect sacrifice and brought us back into divine order and right relationship with our Father.

It is a stunning glimpse of His outrageous desire to know each one of us intimately. A Father who sacrificed His own Son because it was the only thing that could redeem us and restore us? Could you imagine sacrificing your child for a people group who don't even love you in return; they don't understand you, they blaspheme you? God knew someone had to pay the final price for our sins, so we could be brought into the presence of a perfect God. Jesus answered the call; He said "Yes!" He gave His own life so while we were still sinners; we could be cleansed and made righteous in the sight of God our Father. I would say both of them have a radical love for you and me, and for all of creation.

The Bible states in 1 John 4:8 that *"God is love."* It's actually who He is.

First Corinthians 13:4-8 describes love: *"Love is patient, and love is kind. It does not envy, it does not boast, it is not proud. It does not dishonor others, it is not self-seeking, it is not easily angered, it keeps no record of wrongs. Love does not delight in evil but rejoices with the truth. It always protects, always trusts, always hopes, and always perseveres. Love never fails."*

Would you say you know God's love intimately? Do you desire more in your spiritual life than lukewarm Christianity? Do you feel like you know "about God," but don't really *know* God? Maybe you have seen Christianity from afar, and the fruit you see from so-called "Christians" makes you want nothing to do with Jesus? I totally get that. I have walked that path myself. I was and still am appalled and turned off, as well, at the way some self-proclaiming "Christians" act. Can I share a secret with you? True Christ-centered faith is saturated with radical, reckless love (see the definition above). It does not seek its own above another; it meets you right where you are at, and picks you up and carries you to safety! It is a deep intimacy with a loving God who will radically set you free! God wants to restore your hope in humanity; He wants to lavish His free gift of grace upon you and give you the desires of your heart. God *is* truly a good, good Father.

Those bad things you see in society are not God's work! In fact, Jesus states in the book of John, *"I am the Gateway. To enter through me is to experience life, freedom and satisfaction. A thief has only one thing in mind, he wants to steal, slaughter, and destroy. But I have come to give you everything in abundance, more than you expect—life in its fullness until you overflow"* (John 10:9-10). He is looking for you and me to step into our destinies and transform our homes, our churches, our cities, our regions, our nation, and the nations of the world. We have the authority to release the reckless love that is the actual DNA of who God is.

Some believe that God sits on His throne in Heaven and is in charge of all things, good and bad. They tell me they cannot serve a God who allows the evil in this world to go on as it is. Have you ever felt this way? Let's read a few Scriptures together and find out what's really going on, because I think we all know deep down something doesn't feel right about that.

Genesis 1:26 says, *"And God said, Let us (Father, Son, and Holy Spirit) make mankind in Our image, after Our likeness: and let them have complete authority over the fish of the sea and over the birds of the air, the beasts and over all the earth, and over everything that creeps upon the earth."*

The Creator of the world gave mankind (that's you and me) authority over the earth. A pretty high call, actually. It wasn't long before Satan came in whispering twisted ideas and deceiving them. They disobeyed God and partook of the one thing He asked them not to, the Tree of the Knowledge of Good and Evil (Genesis 3). They were banished from the Garden for their own sake, and sin entered into the DNA of man with that one choice to disobey. Perfect intimacy with God the Father was lost, and things went downhill quickly. God wanted man to choose Him, to want Him, so He offered a choice in the garden. A choice to serve Him or to disobey and do their own will.

Our Father, knowing they had a choice to disobey, set a rescue plan in place before the foundation of the world. Jesus, the only Savior, became the perfect sacrifice to redeem mankind and bring them back into fellowship with God. In the beginning of the New Testament, the

Gospels of Matthew, Mark, Luke, and John share the full story of how Jesus gave authority to the disciples. Matthew 10:1 says, *"And He (Jesus) had called his twelve disciples; he gave them power and authority over unclean spirits, to cast them out, and to heal all manner of sickness and all manner of disease."*

Are you struggling or angry with God about the injustice in the world? Are you pushing the blame on Him for not doing something? Friends, He already did something! He gave the church, His bride, the "Ecclesia," the power and authority over unclean spirits and all manner of sickness and disease. These Scriptures declare that the disciples of Jesus have authority over the evil in this world. If you are a disciple of Jesus Christ, you have authority, given by God, to do all that Matthew 10:1 declares.

There is a serious infiltration of evil running rampant in our cities, nation, and throughout the world. But I assure you, God is NOT to blame. It is high time the self-professing Christians (followers of Christ) step into their calling, their destiny, their anointing, and declare the works of Jesus throughout the land! This is a battle cry, a day of beckoning! Inaction in the church has led us to this place. Selfishness has led us to this place. God isn't withholding; He's waiting on the church to awaken, for our hearts to awaken to Truth!

Romans 8 is one of my favorite chapters of the Bible. I shared 8:19 earlier: *"The entire universe is standing on tiptoe, yearning for the unveiling of God's glorious sons and daugh-*

ters!" It continues and says this, in verses 20-21: *"For against its will the universe itself has had to endure the empty futility resulting from the consequences of human sin. But now, with eager expectation, ALL creation longs for the freedom from its slavery to decay and to experience with us the wonderful freedom coming to God's children."*

All of creation is waiting on us, you and me! Creation is crying out, "HELP US! SAVE US! DELIVER US! HEAL US! SET US FREE!" The Holy Spirit is waiting to empower us, to transform us, to give us strength where we are weak! Every detail of our lives is continually woven together to fit God's perfect plan and bring good into our lives, for we are His children who have been called to fulfill His designed purpose. For He knew all about us before we were born. He designed us, from the beginning, to share the likeness of His Son. We are deeply loved. Nothing can separate us from His Love—not death, not life—and nothing has the power to diminish His love towards us. No problems, no trials, no threats... nothing compares to His omnipotent love!

> I decree and declare over you: The chains and fear tactics of the enemy will hold you back no more, in the name of the Lord Jesus Christ. You will run and not grow weary; you will love radically and not grow faint. You will pursue help from the Holy Spirit to walk in your divine calling, in Jesus' name!

Can I share a testimony of what this looks like? I mean everyday life stuff. I was with my husband, three children, and a few friends. We went out to share God's love on the streets one weekend recently. As we were walking into the mall, a young lady was walking out, limping. I immediately knew we were going to pray for this woman. A friend we were with knew the woman and began a conversation with her. She was visibly in pain. He asked her what was going on and told her he would be praying for her (implying in the future, but not in that moment). My husband, with great boldness and a love for this hurting woman, asked if we could pray for her right then. She happily said, "Yes."

Aaron prayed for her, commanding the pain to leave, and immediately her hip was healed, just like that! She was declaring the pain in her hip had left, but that her knees were still hurting so badly. Aaron asked her if I could pray for her. I stepped up to pray for her knees, and as I finished a quick prayer, she instantly bent over, weeping. She was shaking her hands, testing out her knees and hip, and was shocked and emotional at the touch of God that had just taken place. This woman was completely healed in the parking lot, leaving the mall! A few strangers chose to push fear aside and STEP into their authority and take back dominion from the enemy. "Destroying hell for a living," as Todd White calls it. Wow. Praise You, Jesus!! This was such a beautiful touch from the Lord.

To help you understand my mood that day: just that morning I had wanted to veg out and go swimming or go to the zoo with the kids. But instead, the Lord had a divine encounter for us, an encounter with our destinies. Those plans included meeting that young lady. She will never forget that moment when God reached out and touched her through total strangers. This LOVE is what will change our cities, regions, and nation. You and me, coming fully alive in Him and walking in our authority and power in Jesus' name!

We must choose to step into God's empowering grace and walk out His love manifested to the world. This action looks like something—it looks like FREEDOM to everyone we meet! We are called to deny ourselves and follow Him! He is the perfect representation of love.

Things are getting deep, friends. Would you believe there is a sequel to the Reckless Pursuit dream I had? Jump on in, we are about to go swimming!

3

RECKLESS SURRENDER

"The world has not yet seen what God could do with one man who would be totally surrendered to Him. I want to be that man." —D.L. Moody

One month after the Reckless Pursuit dream, I found myself startling awake one morning from another encounter with the Lord. Another prophetic dream, bringing my destiny right into the light!

This dream begins as I am swimming in a small river with my children and a friend of mine. We are swimming up river, when we come to a beautiful waterfall. The river began to rise and waves started to build. My friend asks, "Have you ever swam under a waterfall?" I am immediately startled and terrified. "NO! Who does crazy stuff like that?" I am thinking to myself, "I have a family, and responsibilities, I cannot be so reckless." She giggles (seeing my look of terror) and says,

"Come on" and dives into the water under the waterfall. I panic. I feel like it's a lost cause to stay behind. Drowning in the rising river will become my fate if I remain, and at the same time, I'm terrified to follow her. It truly is a moment of sheer terror, where both decisions seem impossible.

I dive into the water, deep under the waterfall. My eyes open as I am swimming down into this large underwater gathering place. Hundreds of people are there. The water is crystal clear. There are many different dimensions and rooms with tables floating and people around them visiting, laughing, and enjoying one another. I see groups all around, laughing and having so much fun—even my oldest daughter is there. We are swimming so quickly from room to room, deeper and deeper. I lose my swimsuit bottoms and gasp, but they float right back to me. My mind caught up to what I was experiencing and I begin to panic, again, asking my friend, "How are we talking and breathing underwater?"

She and I start swimming upwards to the top; I stop swimming as I see these intersecting cement paths above me. (I gasp.) I see huge bursts of electric voltage pumping back and forth energizing the waters. They were pulsating, and these massive amounts of "life-giving" air were coming out every few seconds, sustaining us while we swam.

I woke up from the dream. I knew immediately I was just looking up at the scene of my first dream a month earlier. There I was beneath the "high voltage" waters, which were being energized by the Spirit of the living God. Beneath the surface was a gathering of people having no cares in the world, breathing perfectly in the depths of His Presence, joyful and free. What I feared the most in my first dream, being pursued and pushed into those high voltage waters, was actually what would give me life today and sustain me.

> "Deep calls to deep in the roar of your waterfalls; all your waves and breakers have swept over me." (Psalm 42:7)

Through this second encounter, this dream, the Lord showed me there was nothing to fear as I laid down my life, fully surrendered, diving in deep to the unknown paths of the Spirit of God.

I was so afraid of losing control and was fighting every step, but for what? A life filled with stress, frustration, and lots of striving? Why would I want to keep that life? Have you ever considered the Scriptures and understood what it means to "surrender your life of selfish ambitions and desires" (James 3:16) and embrace the life God Himself, the Creator of the universe, has for you? Wow, what a humbling and direct confirmation the Lord gave to me through this dream. He is taking my fear and trading it in for strength and courage to run the race He has set before me, completely free in Him! Do you want to know the best part? He urged me to share these dreams with YOU, because He wants the same for you! Let's do this together, my friend!

As I reflect, I believe losing my swimsuit bottoms represents the exposure of my flesh, my weakness. I will be exposed; those who are hungry for more of God and also those who are already submerged in Him will see the struggle of our flesh dying. It is in the LIGHT that darkness is exposed (Ephesians 5:13). Every person experiences this at some point, and those in the dream were neither judging me nor will they judge you as you recklessly surrender to Him. Instead of judgement, they are encouraging us to continue the pursuit because losing our lives for His sake is the only true way to be free!

> "Let me be clear, the Anointed One has set us free—not partially, but completely and wonderfully free! We must always cherish this truth and stubbornly refuse to go back into the bondage of our past." (Galatians 5:1)

To be totally honest, the day we "give our lives to Christ" and are "born again" is also the day we give up our rights. We must deny our own flesh, for we now belong to Him, no longer ourselves. Or maybe you never have truly given your life over to God? Are you doing a very good job at being satisfied and happy on your own? Our Father knows the beginning from the end and He wants to use each of His children to bring healing and life to the nations, which includes YOU! He wants YOU to be safe and secure in His loving hands, healed, delivered from your bondages, and set free. He is looking for sons and daughters who will surrender their lives and be transformed by His love.

If you have never given your life to Jesus, or you have long ago, but you want to surrender it fully to Him today, and you believe Christ died for you, I want to give you that opportunity. Would you agree that everyone is tired of religion and rules, empty words and nagging?

Are you tired of religion stating you must shape up before "God" comes to get you? That is *not* the God I serve, and *not* the God of Abraham, Isaac, and Jacob. My God, Yahweh, is relentless, yes, but in His pursuit for our hearts, He wants to restore us and show us our destiny, not strike us down. We cannot save ourselves, and our good deeds will never earn us a place in the Kingdom of Heaven. We must yield fully to Him; it's that simple.

One night, I was standing in my kitchen preparing dinner for my family, like every other day. I had worship music playing when I heard a new song that energized my spirit. A song that sounded like the very voice of God reading my innermost thoughts...

> "I have come to this place in my life;
> I'm full but I've not satisfied
> this longing to have more of You.
> And I can feel it, my heart is convinced,
> I'm thirsty, my soul can't be quenched.
> You already know this but still,
> come and do whatever You want to..."

(*In Over My Head* by Jenn Johnson)

I listened intently to every word. The captivating way the Spirit of God was calling me deeper with Him into such an intimacy... I truly felt full, and yet not satisfied. I needed more. I had a deep hunger. It required I give up my own will and allow Him to "come and do whatever You want to." As we take each step closer to Him, deeper into the unknown, into the waves of His presence, we experience a brand new thing: losing control, and yet, being set free at the same time.

> "I'm standing knee deep but I'm out where
> I've never been,
> I feel You coming and I hear Your voice on
> the wind,
> Would You come and tear down the boxes
> that I have tried to put You in?
> Let love come teach me who You are again;
> Would You take me back to the place where my
> heart was only about You?
> And all I wanted was just to be with You.
> Come and do whatever You want to."

These verses instantly took me back to my dream of the river rising and the waterfall before me, as I lost control going under the waterfall. It was there that I found freedom in His Spirit. I wasn't free to do my own thing, but free to fulfill my calling and purpose for being on this earth at this moment in time.

> "Then You crash over me and
> I've lost control but I'm free
> I'm going under, I'm in over my head
> You crash over me, I'm where You want me to be
> I'm going under, I'm in over my head
> Whether I sink, whether I swim;
> Oh it makes no difference when
> I'm beautifully in over my head."

It's time to dive into the water with me, and let His waters cleanse you and purify you! Whether we sink or whether we swim, it really makes no difference if we are with Him. Will you allow Him to put off all the unrighteous deeds and be made new in Him? Jesus paid for every sin, every mistake you and I have ever made, and all you have to do is simply say, "YES! I want You, Jesus. I want You to have my old life and give me a new one. Restore me!"

Father, I just thank You for Your reckless pursuit of not just myself, but each person reading this. Your love continues to overwhelm me. We repent before You, Lord, for all the ways we have tried to do this on our own and failed. We repent for not seeking You, for not trusting You. We repent for not being surrendered to You. Father we just thank you right now, for sending Your perfect

Son, Jesus, to die for us on the cross. We thank You that He carried all our sin, and paid the greatest price to set us free. On this day we surrender our own will, our entire life to You, we confess with our mouth You are our Lord, You alone are our Savior, and we thank You for washing our sins clean with Your righteousness. We renounce and leave behind any deeds of darkness, and step into Your glorious light in Jesus name.

Holy Spirit, we ask You to touch each of us, overwhelm us with Your presence and power. Fill us, Holy Spirit; we say yes to You. Have Your way in us, mold us, shape us, prune us, and help us look like Jesus more and more each day. Thank You for changing the desires of our hearts to match Your plans for us. Thank You for allowing us to hear You clearly and be trained up in the Spirit. God, we honor You and thank You for never giving up on us, for never saying we aren't worth the trouble anymore. You amaze us; we love You so much! In Jesus' name, amen.

Wow! Wonderful! Glorious! If you said this prayer and surrendered your life today, you are now a child of God; Welcome to our Kingdom Family! (*Please connect with me and let me know. I'd love to hear from you and help you get connected with some great resources!*)

4

RECKLESS OBEDIENCE

"Don't just listen to the Word of Truth and not respond to it, for that is the essence of self-deception. So always let His Word become like poetry written and fulfilled by your life."
—James 1:22

Before you close the book here, may I remind you, I think we all have issues with obedience. We have been hurt in the past, or we just lack the self-control to follow through with what we have been asked of the Lord to do! This is not a good enough reason to give up! In fact, the more you struggle, the more of an assault on your destiny. The enemy is fighting hard to keep you from obeying the Lord's commands, because he fears what you will do in God's strength! I'll share my own struggles to help you understand, and we can walk this out together!

My old nature/flesh (before Christ transformed me)

was a type A personality—a control freak through and through, with a deep base of fear of the unknown. Some of you are nodding your head. You know someone just like that, or maybe you are that someone. Do not fear. There is hope for every personality type. Many of you have reached out to me and asked what has changed in me and why I am so different now. You have asked how you can find peace and trust the Lord more fully.

Can I be vulnerable again with you? I am still learning. I still freak out. Under pressure, I clam up, and I simply bite my tongue and cry out for the Holy Spirit to invade me and HELP! You and I are a work in progress, and we will grow from glory to glory (2 Corinthians 3:18). We are stepping up a level at a time, growing in intimacy and looking more like Jesus each day, as a PROCESS. So, promise me this, do not beat yourself up. We need and have the body of Christ, brothers and sisters, to walk alongside us and lift us up higher as we make this journey.

As a full time mama to three growing children, I have learned each day that I am stepping into a classroom. God is training me and teaching me through these little people who look up to me and think I have it all together. I can brand them with religious rules and demands, as can you with your children or those in your realm of influence. But in my pursuit of raising Spirit-led children, rather than forcing them to obey my demands, I found deep revelation from the Lord in this Scripture:

"For God has not given us a spirit of fear, but of power, love and *self*-control." (2 Timothy 1:7)

The Fruit of the Spirit (Galatians 5) includes self-control, as well. Through continued intimacy with the Holy Spirit, He showed me we were never created to control others, nor does God control us. The Fruit of the Spirit of God that dwells in every born again believer is actually *self*-control. The feelings we can experience to control situations are actually given to us by God, BUT they are given to control *ourselves*, not others, and not the Holy Spirit! You and I are created to use *self*-control and deny ourselves the desires of the flesh and seek first the Kingdom. As we do, ALL we need will be added unto us (Matthew 6:33)! We control and deny ourselves and let the Holy Spirit move and have His way in us.

Part of this revelation is not allowing others to control us in return. People, unwillingly and sometimes willingly, will try to run your life and steal your time. They will demand from you things you know you are not called to do. Part of the revelation of "self-control" the Lord showed me is that I am to serve Him only, and not man. I cannot be afraid to tell someone no. We cannot be men-pleasers and also please God.

I'm not sure about you, but I have many jobs: running several ministries with my husband, homeschooling our three children, hosting a podcast, writing books, and don't forget leading an incredible team of hundreds (soon to be thousands) of entrepreneurs through my at-home business. If you and I want to fulfill the true purpose we are on this planet, at this point in history, we must really know what our vision and calling from God is. Do you realize it's impossible to have great vision from the Lord and not say no to other opportunities—often?

In order for me to do all God has called me to, I must steward my time incredibly well and follow that vision God gave me. You and I must be intentional and help equip only those He calls us to help. In this way, we can inspire whoever is in front of us to seek an intimate relationship with God as well, so they do not look just to us to fulfill their needs. I am very passionate about helping each one of you simplify your own life by catching the personal vision God has for you. When we know this, we know exactly what to do and what not to do. A huge part of the ministry and business I have includes training others how to walk fully in their destiny.

> "Am I now trying to win the approval of human beings, or of God? Or am I trying to please people? If I were still trying to please people, I would not be a servant of Christ." (Galatians 1:10)

I feel like that is pretty clearly defined. We must seek His face and do only what the Father is doing. Jesus said that He only says what the Father is saying and does what the Father is doing. We are to be His disciples and follow

His leading. Equipping others to do the same is truly the bread and butter of the Gospel! Teaching and training others to set healthy boundaries in their relationships and protect their time and steward well the talents, gifts, and people that God has given each of us to steward is key to living a balanced, fulfilling life.

In John 15, Jesus describes what a living vine looks like. He says we must remain in fellowship with Him. If we try to go off on our own, our branch is severed from the vine and will not bear fruit. Our lives will be fruitless unless we stay intimately joined to His vine, where all life flows. In verse 14, Jesus declares that we prove we are His intimate friends when we obey all that He has commanded us to do.

So, friend, prepare your heart right now for a season of not pleasing man, but surrendering that need of approval, only for God. If you choose to take this journey, I promise you will find incredible freedom! The kind of freedom that will give you the courage to stay home Thanksgiving weekend, all alone, hidden away in your office and write a book the Lord told you to write. Without having discipline and stewarding God's heart well, we won't be able to accomplish what He has asked us to do.

Jesus says in John 15:12-13, *"So this is my command: Love each other deeply, as much as I have loved you. For the greatest love of all is a love that sacrifices all..."*

Obedience will not always be painful, let me be clear.

Often times, it will give us the greatest joy to sacrifice our plans and see God's love overwhelm the one in front of us. Our obedience to Christ alone will give us wings to fly, and He will lead us through doors no man can shut, and open our spirit and heart to truly love the least of these. God is not looking for perfect people; He is seeking willing, teachable vessels He can work and move through. I should be a great example of that. My past does not define me, and your past does not define you. We become new creations, because of Jesus Christ, as we repent from sin and turn back to Him. Be assured He wants to use you, dear friend, to transform those around you and lead them into the *freedom* only found in a surrendered life before the Lord Jesus Christ.

I decree and declare over you radical, quick obedience in your walk with Christ. You will hear clearly the Father's voice, discern His plans and calling on your life, and quickly obey each step of the way, in Jesus' name.

RECKLESS ABANDON

"The only way people come to me is by the Father who sent me—He pulls on their hearts to embrace me. And those who are drawn to me, I will certainly raise them up in the last day." —John 6:44

When we surrender to Christ, we are giving in to the drawing of the Holy Spirit. Our surrender is a release of our will into His. A reckless abandon, on the other hand, is even more intense. Abandon is deeper, and is not just a giving into a pressure, but the giving up of something.

In the introduction, I shared with you how I recalled a shift when my family moved back to Kansas when I was in elementary school. Just so it's clear, I have the most amazing parents. When God called them to leave

Tennessee, my oldest brother and brand new wife did not move with us. As the pastors, they were not only leaving a church family, but part of their own family behind. I was too young to really understand at the time the challenge and heartache this caused them. However, they were obedient to the Lord through the pain.

In that season of deep transition and grieving, they gave of themselves so fully to the Lord. I thought they were crazy back then, but I see what they did as admirable now. They began the process of becoming foster parents upon arriving in Kansas. They bought an old church building and remodeled and began fixing it up. Soon this church which my parents turned into a home would house the many, many foster children who would come to live with us over the years, three of whom would become my adopted sisters.

This time was very challenging for me. While my parents were very busy helping these children who lived in our home, the enemy saw a perfect opportunity to capture me. If you recall, I shared briefly on the wayward years, and one day I may share my full testimony. During this time, I allowed the enemy to whisper lies and steal my hope and my future right out from beneath me. My hometown became the location of my greatest trauma, rebellion, sin, and ultimately, the loss of my identity in Christ. I truly wanted to run away and never return. When we run, we don't have to face our past, right?

I somehow graduated high school and moved away to college, as far away as I could possibly endure. I was sure I would never return to the city of my youth. In fact, it would take me some 15 years to return for more than a quick visit to see my family. During those years, I married an amazing man, had three wonderful children, and somehow found my way back to Jesus. Actually, I became pretty desperate for Him. I found myself in such a place of *recklessly surrendering* to the Lord that I told God I would go ANYWHERE and do anything for Him. What I didn't realize was that in order to fulfill that call, I would literally have to abandon everything I was holding onto.

In June 2015, the Lord spoke to my husband and gave clear direction that we were to return to my hometown. Before I really thought this through, I *recklessly abandoned* all I'd held onto—all the anger, the fear, everything. I said "Yes!" Literally, ten days later, our family of five and a brand new puppy packed all we had. We set off with less than $1,000 in the bank. No jobs on the other side. But our hearts were FULLY HIS!

I'm not sure if you know this or not, but God is super into restoring that which was lost! He took me into a safe place to heal during those years away from my hometown. I healed just enough to say "YES," and then He sent me back, so He could restore my identity. Great amounts of freedom took place in me spiritually as we returned not just to my hometown, but to live in *the very home* I grew up in. There were many tears and great trials. I stood face to face with so many giants that I thought I would turn and run, but instead, in the strength of the Lord Jesus Christ, I whipped out Scriptural truth like rocks and nailed those giants right in the forehead! I pushed through the spirit of fear, and I faced each day with a determination and a renewed HOPE.

Because I'm sure you want to hear some great stories and testimonies, I will humor you. I recall during pre-marital counseling, telling Aaron several things I would never do. I would never move to western Kansas (where we shortly thereafter lived for TEN years) and I would never be a pastor's wife. All the while, *both* of these things I would come face to face with when we returned to my hometown and I had to face my past. There was no more running, and the shame came in strong. As the Lord called us to plant a church, in the very place I ran away from so many years ago, a giant was slain by our obedience. As He called me to become a "pastor's wife," another giant was slain. As I eventually stepped into the role and pastored and preached myself, *as a woman*, more religious giants were slain. My shame from the past was put into the purifying fire, and I came out healed, not even smelling like smoke.

> "God is not looking for golden vessels or silver vessels.
> He is looking for willing vessels." —**Kathryn Kuhlman**

Please hear my heart: if He can use me, He can use ANYONE! He is simply looking for *willing* vessels, those who will say "Yes" to Him. Would you dare to step into the unknown? Would you press through your fears and any shame from the past and consider accepting the invitation?

This is where you simply *must* grab your Bible. Open up to Isaiah 61, one of my favorite chapters of all time. I'll share a little, but take the time and read the entire chapter. While you do, let God's presence just wash over you. Allow the abundant favor of Jesus Christ to consume your innermost being.

This is *our* story! This is beauty for ashes, restoration and freedom for ourselves, and once we are healed, this is our commission to the lost and hurting world:

> "The Spirit of the Sovereign Lord is on me,
> because the Lord has anointed me to proclaim
> the good news to the poor. He has sent me to
> bind up the brokenhearted,
> to proclaim freedom for the captives,
> and release from darkness for the prisoners,
> to proclaim the year of the Lord's favor
> and the day of vengeance of our God;
> to comfort all who mourn,
> and provide for those who grieve in Zion—
> to bestow on them a crown of beauty
> instead of ashes, the oil of joy instead of

mourning; and a garment of praise
instead of a spirit of despair.
They will be called oaks of righteousness,
a planting of the Lord, for the display of his
splendor. They will rebuild the ancient ruins
and restore the places long devastated;
they will renew the ruined cities that have been
devastated for generations.
Strangers will shepherd your flocks;
foreigners will work your fields and vineyards.
And you will be called priests of the Lord,
you will be named ministers of our God.
You will feed on the wealth of nations,
and in their riches you will boast.
Instead of your shame you will receive a double
portion, and instead of disgrace
you will rejoice in your inheritance.
And so you will inherit a double portion
in your land, and everlasting joy will be yours.
'For I, the Lord, love justice;
I hate robbery and wrongdoing.'"
(Isaiah 61:1-8)

In our *reckless abandon*, our Father can use us to take back our families from the enemy's hands. In our *reckless abandon*, God will use us to free our cities from the oppression of hell. In our *reckless abandon*, Holy Spirit will show us we won't only take back our cities but the region, the nation, and the nations of the world.

It is through this process—His reckless pursuit, His reckless love, our reckless obedience, our reckless surrender, our reckless abandon—that we will leave the dry and weary desert once and for all, and *truly* enter into our Promised Land.

RECKLESSLY PURSUE THE PROMISED LAND

"For you reach into my heart. With one flash of your eyes I am undone by your love, my beloved, my equal, my bride. You leave me breathless..." —***Song of Songs 4:9***

The most beautiful scene flooded my mind the day I opened my brand new Passion Translation Bible. As you know, I was raised in church; however, there was one book of the Bible I am not sure I had ever read before. It was simply too risky, too vivid and expressive for my understanding. However, when my new Bible came, the Holy Spirit encouraged me to start there, the very Song of Songs (Solomon) as it is called in The Passion Translation.

The poetic response back and forth between the bride of Christ (you and me) and her bridegroom (Jesus) is truly the most breathtaking, divine romance story ever written. It was a deep calling to deep encounter between the King of all the universe and me. I was truly wrecked in every sense of the word. My perspective of how adoring and in love with me Jesus really is forever changed me. If you don't have a copy of this translation, I highly recommend it. It has allowed the Scriptures to come alive in a new way for me.

Here is a little backstory so you can walk this journey with me:

At the beginning of 2018, I felt called into my first extended Daniel Fast. I had fasted a few meals here and there in the past, but this was different. During this time, I had a deep revelation of how God called the Israelites out of Egypt to a very special place to worship Him. Where was this place? I answered, "The Promised Land." And yet, that's not what the Scriptures say. God actually calls them out of Egypt and into the *desert* to worship Him. In the desert, the tough place, the dry and barren place, the Lord wished to meet His people and encounter them. He wanted to become *ALL* they needed. He desired that they become satisfied with Him and Him alone in that place. God wanted them to find His presence and allow His presence to lead them into the Promised Land, flowing with milk and honey.

There is no place for murmuring or complaining in His presence, and finding joy in ALL THINGS is, in fact, what accelerates us into our Promised Land. I truly was undone as I realized why not just myself, but so many others spend so long in the wilderness, wandering around and around like the Israelites did for forty years. They spent *forty* years grumbling and complaining about their situation. A journey that should have taken them less than two weeks cost them *forty* years. And very few got to inherit that Promised Land, if you recall. Very few ever had revelation of who God truly was, how powerful and incredible He is.

I realized in that moment that our Father is drawing us out into the desert to be with Him. He is longing for us; He wants to restore our relationship to how it was in the Garden before Adam and Eve gave it all away. As we seek His face, as you and I come into the secret place with Him, *He* actually becomes our Promised Land. *HE DOES!* Our intimacy with our Father becomes that Promised Land we have been seeking all this time! I assure you, nothing else will satisfy. Nothing we desire can satisfy like the sweet presence of our Father in Heaven. He is calling us into intimacy and in that secret place alone will we become truly undone and perfected by His Presence.

I was reading in Song of Songs, from start to finish, embracing the notes and going deep with the Lord as I read the most beautiful love story of ALL love stories. Jesus, the Bridegroom, is speaking of the beauty of His bride (that's you and me, friend) and saying how we leave Him breathless, how merely a glance from our worshipping eyes steal His heart.

> "Your loving words are like the honeycomb to me; your tongue releases milk and honey, for I find the Promised Land flowing from within you." (Song of Songs 4:11)

In the notes, it says, "Both the Promised Land and your heart flow with milk and honey. *You* have become the Promised Land of Jesus Christ."

Back up, rewind. "*I* have become the Promised Land of Jesus Christ?" I found myself weeping in His presence, completely undone.

As we seek His Presence, He becomes *our* Promised Land. This alone is beautiful, mind blowing. But can you even fathom this?! That *we*, you and me, have become *the* Promised Land of our Lord Jesus Christ? The Savior of the world, who sacrificed everything, gave all He had. He surrendered His Kingship. He left His throne in Heaven. He was born of a virgin. He came into this corrupt world and walked this earth as a man, not God. He faced every challenge we face, yet stayed sinless. Though betrayal, being treated unfairly, lied about, cursed, and beaten, He *still* gave His very life. He allowed His blood to run freely to cleanse and purify you and me. *We* are His Promised Land, *His greatest desire*!

That, my friend, *IS* the greatest love story ever written. Period. End of Story.

> Our Promised Land is not a place or a destination. It is a person, one person, the Lord Jesus Christ.

Once we find our Promised Land, we find our calling and our destiny. We can find our people group, our tribe, and our heart's desires will be fulfilled. In Hebrews 12: 1-2, it says, *"Jesus endured the cross, for the joy set before him."* We were the joy set before Him; being able to be in relationship with us is why He surrendered everything and set us free.

The prophetic is one of the most amazing tools for helping lead others into their identity and destiny in Jesus Christ! Shawn Bolz, host of Exploring the Prophetic, says, "When we fall in love with our people group, provision will come." I believe the prophetic call on my life is what brought me "home." It was this prophetic call that brought me back to my hometown in 2015 so Jesus could redeem that which was lost. He redeemed my calling and destiny. In the process, God has given me such a love for my hometown, such a desire to see this city radically set free and on fire for Jesus Christ! I have cultivated a love in my heart to see the very city and the very people that once robbed me of my identity, set free.

It is the very essence of why we are alive today; we must love outrageously and show others their Kingdom identity and calling! It's simply put, the Great Commission: *"As you go into all the world, preach openly the wonderful news of the gospel to the entire human race!" (Mark 16:15)*.

Who are you drawn to? Who do you feel a connection

with? What type of people do you enjoy helping? Often our "people group" includes those who have been where we once were, those seeking the breakthroughs we have already found. We hold a great authority to help others through trials once we have received our own breakthrough. For example, if you have been through a tragedy and healed, you have the means to help others overcome in that area. If you have been through a struggle of any kind, and have broken through and been victorious, you hold Kingdom authority to help others break through their similar struggle. They will trust you, and you will understand them. These very people are often your "people group." It's time to make a plan to help not only yourself, but your people group reach their fullest potential! When we find our calling and purpose, we will find great provision from the Lord.

You have all the tools to do this if you are fully surrendered to the Lordship of Jesus Christ! If you are filled with the Holy Spirit of the Living God, you are now equipped with power and you are destined to change the world! Do not delay one more minute! Go share what Jesus has done for you! Give away the hope that you have. Remember, *all* of creation is waiting on the sons and daughters of God to step into their true identity and bring the Kingdom of Heaven to this earth. *You* have been called.

Will *you* accept your call, and step into your destiny?

7

PRACTICAL STEPS AND DECREES TO ENTER INTO THE PROMISED LAND

Here's the thing: God wants to know *you*. He wants to talk to *you*. He wants to spend time with *you*. I hope you fully understand this. Please say "Yes!" I pray I haven't spent all this time with you just for you to be stuck thinking intimacy with Jesus isn't for *you*.

Here are a few simple and practical ways to grow in relationship with Him:

1) LOOK FOR HIM ALL AROUND YOU

Listen for His voice. He speaks to me in many different ways: nature, my children/others, music, dreams, visions, the Bible, books, movies, encouragement from a friend, His own audible voice, a "knowing" in my spirit (or a peace that something is correct/wrong), etc. If we are listening and are looking for Him, we WILL find Him and hear Him.

> "Don't limit God to fit in the way that you think that He is going to speak, because just about the time that we think we have Him figured out, He will oftentimes speak to us in another way. God wants us to be in tune with Him, and not just in tune with one of the ways that He gives those words." —**Randy Clark**

2) SPEND TIME IN QUIET

Did you know if the enemy can't convince you to believe lies, he will keep you so darn busy you won't ever have time to seek the Lord's will for your life. Being busy is *not* admirable; it is part of the enemy's plot to keep you from your destiny. Trust me, I have tended to be a BUSY BEE, and I learned this first hand. We should be intentional and work hard and as unto the Lord in all we do, but this is much different from just keeping your mind and body busy going to and fro always. Remember the Sabbath day? We are designed to rest, and spend time with Him. How can you carve out quiet time with the Lord? I get up early before my children and husband wake, read my Bible and journal and pray. To become intimate with our Father, we should desire to spend time with Him daily! He truly is our daily bread.

3) JOURNAL

Journaling is one of my favorite ways to practice hearing His voice and also recording the testimonies of how He has come through and answered my prayers! When I am struggling and feel far from Him, I open my journal and remind myself of His goodness in my life. I am almost always immediately taken into His presence and blessed—even on the worst days, this works. Go buy a journal now, or grab a notebook, and try this, even for two weeks, and see how much of a difference it makes to get your thoughts out on paper. A new believer, a macho guy I know, said he used to think journaling was so stupid, until he tried it, and saw how the Lord transformed his thinking and showed him His goodness! Even guys can journal. My husband does as well; he's not as wordy as me, but nonetheless, he journals.

4) STAY CONNECTED TO THE VINE

Anything we begin in our flesh will end in the flesh. But what begins by the Spirit of God will last! Remember the Vine and the branches. We will not have lasting fruit apart from the True Vine: Jesus. We can take an idea the Lord has given us and try to force it and make it happen in our own strength, or we can continue to surrender to Him and rest, waiting upon and seeking direction and wisdom. When we rest and trust His timing, often we will receive a shortcut that leads to great success! Matthew 6:33 says, *"Seek first His Kingdom and His righteousness, and all we need will be added unto us."*

5) SURRENDER ALREADY!

Do you know why we continue to waste time in our own strength trying to get what we want, when our true happiness and provision is found only in seeking God's face and submitting to His Spirit? We must surrender and live as the supernatural beings we were created to be. The result will be a life of rest and peace no matter what our circumstances are around us.

The Apostle Paul says, in Philippians 4:11-13 (NIV), *"I am not saying this because I am in need, for I have learned to be content whatever the circumstances. I know what it is to be in need, and I know what it is to have plenty. I have learned the secret of being content in any and every situation, whether well fed or hungry, whether living in plenty or in want. I can do all this through him who gives me strength."*

When Paul wrote this letter to the church at Philippi, he was not only in prison, but his feet were bound. I read once that during these times, the prison cells were below the city, next to the sewage drain systems. Could you imagine being content, bound in prison, with raw sewage running by as you praise and worship Jesus? Paul and Silas were praising and singing to the Most High God when a tremendous miracle occurred. An earthquake shook the foundations and the prison doors were flung open and their chains came loose. The jailor turned to Paul and Silas and asked, "What must I do to be saved?" What a beautiful story of putting one's faith in Jesus Christ.

6) TRAIN YOURSELF TO HEAR GOD'S VOICE

I had a friend refer to me and some others as, "You people." It kind of stopped me in my thoughts, and I said, "Hey, what do you mean by that?" She explained that those who are discerning and know confidently the will of God in situations make her a little nervous and can be intimidating. I totally grasp that. I do. I just explained to her that I was there once, not long ago.

Sweet sister, dear brother...we all begin in the same place—lost, cut off from our Heavenly Father, desperately needing to be reunited. We all have to learn to hear the Lord's voice and discern whether it's our own or His. We just have to practice and seek His face and go with it and try it out. Eventually, we will be so secure in knowing it is Him, we will have no doubts. *"My Sheep will know my voice and a stranger they will not follow"* (John 10:4-5).

There are life and death types of situations where you really need to know the will of God, and it is a good idea to practice hearing His voice long before that, my friends. So start with the small things, simple matters that won't really matter in the realm of eternity. (Should I go to

Walmart or the grocery store? Should I choose chocolate milk or white milk?)

Then, when you're in a situation like I was last year, and your spouse literally gives you five minutes of quiet time and asks you to seek the Lord and ask if you should go on the biggest, most intense mission trip of your lifetime to Africa, you can shut all your emotions and thoughts off and just hear God clearly. Friends, that day, with such a huge decision on the line, I was actually stuffing my face with Oreos and milk and feeling so distant from God when Aaron asked me that question. Guess what, though? The Holy Spirit meets us when we seek His face. He wants to communicate with us; the question is, will we do the work to get to know Him? It's that simple.

In case you were wondering, He gave me a clear answer (I was shocked, actually), but when the pressure was on, He had refined me enough that a diamond shone through in that moment, and I heard His voice clearly tell me, *"Yes! I want you to go!"* The next day, I was asking for confirmation, and I looked at the clock and it was 12:22. This number He has assigned to me, a number which signifies His provision (not just financially, but spiritually, emotionally, physically, all of it!) Luke 12:22 says, *"Never let anxiety enter your hearts. Never worry about any of your needs, such as food or clothing."* I was so overwhelmed by His goodness. He came and met me where I was at, and loved me, and answered me in the special way He always does.

The very song that came on my playlist the night God told me to write *this* book became a confirmation song, as well. The song "Yes & Amen" spoke to me from 1 Corinthians 1:20, *"For all of God's promises find their 'yes' of fulfillment in him. And as his 'yes' and our 'amen' ascend to God, we bring him glory!"* This song and Scripture verse became another way God spoke to me in that season. I heard it again when I was praying about the opportunity to go to Africa. I believe He was making sure I understood His answer, His promise. He was reminding me HE put the desires into my heart to take a mission trip that would absolutely change my life forever. He spoke to my heart and said, "I know you are scared, but I know the beginning from the end." He knew I was worried about my children staying behind, and He assured me they would be safe and He would comfort them.

Do you want to feel that kind of confirmation from Him? It just takes stewarding that time with Him. Even if it's just five minutes, make it count! Ask Him things and then be quiet and listen to what He puts into your heart. And allow Him to speak to you through nature, numbers, visions, peace in your heart, words that just pop into your mind, other people, prophetic words, Scripture, or music. Just be open to hear His edifying and building up! Line everything up with Scripture, God will never go against what Scripture says. If it isn't edifying you or building you up, it is likely the stranger's voice (the enemy) and we should not follow that voice. I believe in you, and I know you can do this!

> "So then faith comes by hearing, and hearing by the word of God" (Rom. 10:17). Notice it does not say, faith comes from having heard. The whole nature of faith implies a relationship with God that is current. The emphasis is on hearing...in the now!" —**Bill Johnson**

I will leave you with this last bit of encouragement. If there is any shred of doubt left in you as you finish this book, take this prophetic word I was given and make it your own.

The entire church had been through the prayer line at the end of a conference. Every last single person, including my husband, had been prayed over. I was the only one left. Two mighty men of God and prophetic voices of our day, Adrian Beale and Adam Thompson (The Dream Team), were prophesying after an amazing weekend of meetings.

As I stepped up into view, out of the crowd, Adam chuckled, and said, "Oh, yes! You!" He went on to say how not only my husband, but Jesus adored and loved me. He told me how desperately Jesus wanted to be with me. He wanted a deeper intimacy with me. He longed for me, and he told me because of the call on Aaron's and my lives, there was going to be so much I was going to have to bear. The more time I spent with Jesus, the more I would be able to carry. Even though I felt I was carrying a lot at the time, there was going to be much more weight; the weight of the *very Glory of God*. As I was able to bear more of the glory, we would see miraculous and amazing things manifest in our lives and through our ministry.

I cannot tell you another prophetic word that gripped my heart so strongly. This word put the Holy Fear of God in me. Immediately, I laid down everything on the altar before the Lord, and sought His face, day and night for months. That reckless surrender and abandoning of every "busy work" included every person and thing I elevated above and before my relationship with Jesus. This word forever changed me. The obedience to surrender fully to Jesus forever changed me. I promise you, it will forever change *you*, as well.

Guess what? You don't need to read another book, hear another sermon, or get another prophetic word; you need to *Recklessly Surrender* today, and enter into Your Promised Land. You have the fullness of Christ in you, today.

Enter in.

CONNECT WITH BETH:

Are you ready to catch your God Vision, Simplify Your Life, or maybe even take a guided journey into wellness and abundance—both naturally and spiritually??

Grab a **FREE** Gift to help you get started today at:
www.reckless-surrender.com

To invite Beth for a speaking engagement or training workshop, please contact her at the following:

Email: bethpackard@gmail.com
Online: www.bethpackard.com

Connect on Social:

Facebook @ Super-Natural Living with Beth Packard
Youtube @Beth Packard
Podcast @ Super-Natural Living with Beth Packard